NO-SEW FL_____
THROWS & PILLOWS

LEISURE ARTS, INC
Little Rock, Arkansas

Floral Braided Edge Throw

Approximate Finished Size: 48" x 53"

SHOPPING LIST

- ☐ 1⅝ yards **each** of two contrasting fleeces
- ☐ masking tape

To make the throw:

1. Cut the fleece pieces to 51" x 56" each. Stack the fleece pieces **wrong** sides together.
2. Place masking tape strips 1½" in from all four sides. Cutting through both layers, cut 1" wide x 1½" deep fringe along all four sides of each fleece piece *(Fig. 1)*. Remove the tape.

Fig. 1

1½"

1½

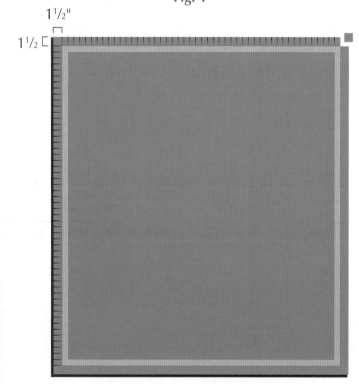

3. Cut slits in each fringe piece on all four sides of each fleece piece *(Fig. 2)*.

Fig. 2

½"

½"

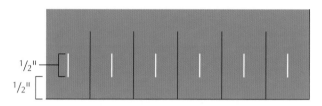

4. Alternating between the top and bottom fleece pieces, pull the fringe pieces through the slits *(Figs. 3-4)*. When you get to the starting point, cut the last piece in half lengthwise and tie a knot.

Fig. 3

Fig. 4

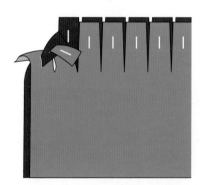

Flames Tied Throw

Approximate Finished Size:
48" x 53", excluding fringe

SHOPPING LIST

☐ 1⁷⁄₈ yards **each** of two contrasting fleeces
☐ masking tape

To make the throw:

1. Cut the fleece pieces to 58" x 63" each. Stack the fleece pieces **wrong** sides together.
2. Place masking tape strips 5" in from all four sides. Cutting through both layers, cut 1" wide x 5" deep fringe along all four sides of each fleece piece *(Fig. 1)*. Remove the tape.

Fig. 1

5"

5"

3. Using one fringe strip from each fleece piece, tie twisted knots (page 30) all the way around the throw.

Checkered Flag Pillow

Approximate Finished Size:
18" square, excluding fringe

SHOPPING LIST

☐ two 22" fleece squares
☐ 18" square pillow form
☐ masking tape

To make the pillow:

1. Stack the fleece pieces **wrong** sides together.
2. Place masking tape strips 2" in from all four sides. Cutting through both layers, cut 1" wide x 2" deep fringe along all four sides of each fleece piece *(Fig. 1)*. Remove the tape.

Fig. 1

2"

2"

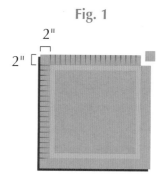

3. Using one fringe strip from each fleece piece, tie knots along three sides. Insert the pillow form in the pillow and tie knots along the fourth side.

Cupcakes Tied Throw

Approximate Finished Size:
48" x 53", excluding fringe

SHOPPING LIST

- ☐ 1⅞ yards **each** of two contrasting fleeces
- ☐ masking tape

To make the throw:

1. Cut the fleece pieces to 58" x 63" each. Stack the fleece pieces **wrong** sides together.
2. Place masking tape strips 5" in from all four sides. Cutting through both layers, cut ½" wide x 5" deep fringe along all four sides of each fleece piece *(Fig. 1)*. Remove the tape.

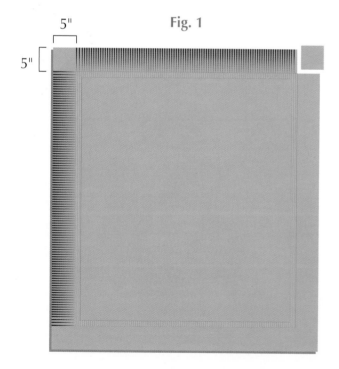

Fig. 1

5"

5"

3. Using one strip from each fleece piece, tie twisted knots (page 30) all the way around the throw.

"Candy" Pillow

Approximate Finished Size: 14" diameter

SHOPPING LIST

- ☐ 34" fleece square for pillow
- ☐ 14" fleece square for pillow back
- ☐ 18" fleece square for candy stripes
- ☐ 36" square of white tulle
- ☐ two 22" ribbon lengths (we used ⅝" wide ribbon)
- ☐ 14" round pillow form
- ☐ fabric marker
- ☐ thumbtack
- ☐ rubber band
- ☐ fabric glue
- ☐ tracing paper
- ☐ string

To make the pillow:

1. For the pillow, match the **right** sides and fold the 34" fleece square in half from top to bottom and again from left to right. Tie one end of a length of string to the fabric marker; insert a thumbtack through the string at 16". Insert the thumbtack through the folded fleece corner. Holding the tack in place and keeping the string taut, mark the cutting line *(Fig. 1)*. Cut out the circle. Repeat to cut a 12½" circle for the pillow back, placing the thumbtack 6¼" from the marker.

Fig. 1

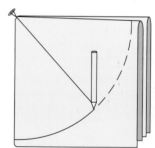

2. Center the pillow form on the **wrong** side of the large fleece circle. Gather the fleece around the pillow form and secure with the rubber band *(Photo 1)*. To finish the pillow back, flatten the gathers and glue the 12½" fleece circle to the pillow over the gathers.

3. Trace the candy stripe pattern (page 31) onto tracing paper and cut out. Use the pattern to cut 4 stripes. Glue the stripes to the pillow.

4. Wrap the pillow in the tulle and tie the ends with the ribbons.

Photo 1

Square Dot Pillow

*Approximate Finished Size:
18" square, excluding fringe*

SHOPPING LIST

- ☐ two 26" fleece squares
- ☐ 18" square pillow form
- ☐ masking tape

To make the pillow:

1. Stack the fleece pieces ***wrong*** sides together.
2. Place masking tape strips 4" in from all four sides. Cutting through both layers, cut ³/₄" wide x 4" deep fringe along all four sides of each fleece piece ***(Fig. 1)***. Remove the tape.

Fig. 1

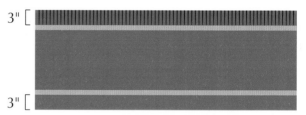

3. Using one fringe strip from each fleece piece and tying each knot twice, tie knots along three sides. Insert the pillow form and tie the fourth side.

Striped Throw

*Approximate Finished Size:
54" x 70", excluding fringe*

SHOPPING LIST

- ☐ ⁵/₈ yard **each** of five contrasting fleeces
- ☐ masking tape

To make the throw:

1. Cut each fleece piece to 54" x 20".
2. Place a masking tape strip 3" in from each long side on one fleece piece. Cut ³/₄" wide x 3" deep fringe along both sides of the fleece piece ***(Fig. 1)***. Remove the tape. Repeat to cut the fringe on the remaining fleece pieces.

Fig. 1

3. Using one fringe strip from each fleece piece, tie twisted knots (page 30) to join two pieces along one long edge. Repeat to join the remaining pieces to the throw.
4. Tie knots along the top and bottom edges.

Rag-Tied "Quilt"

Approximate Finished Size: 70" x 80", excluding fringe; fits a twin size bed

SHOPPING LIST

- ☐ 1½ yards **each** of 8 contrasting fleeces for the quilt
- ☐ ½ yard of contrasting fleece for fringe on the outer edges
- ☐ masking tape

To make the throw:

1. For the fringe on the outer edges, cut 240 ⁵⁄₈" x 4" strips from the fringe fleece; set aside.
2. For the quilt, cut seven 16" squares from each fleece piece.
3. Place masking tape strips 3" in from all four sides on a 16" fleece square. Cut ⁵⁄₈" wide x 3" deep fringe along all four sides *(Fig. 1)*. Repeat on all 56 fleece squares, making the same number of cuts on all sides of all squares. Remove the tape.

Fig. 1

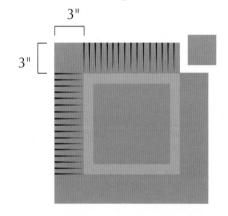

4. Referring to the Diagram for color placement, use twisted knots (page 30) to tie the squares together first in rows and then to join the rows.

Diagram

5. On the outer quilt edges, use two adjacent fringe strips to tie knots, catching a contrasting fringe strip in each knot.

Other Bed Sizes:

Full/Queen *(finished size: 80" x 90", excluding fringe)* 1½ yards each of 8 contrasting fleeces and ½ yard of fleece for contrasting fringe; cut 72 squares and 272 fringe strips

King *(finished size: 90" x 100", excluding fringe)* 1⁷⁄₈ yards each of 8 contrasting fleeces and ½ yard of fleece for contrasting fringe; cut 90 squares and 304 fringe strips

Chevron Bolster Pillow

Approximate Finished Size:
15" x 6", excluding fringe

SHOPPING LIST

- ☐ 26" fleece square for pillow
- ☐ scrap of contrasting fleece for ties
- ☐ 15" x 6" bolster pillow form
- ☐ masking tape
- ☐ 2 rubber bands

To make the pillow:

1. For the pillow, place a masking tape strip 3" in from each side edge on the pillow fleece piece. Cut ¼" wide x 3" deep fringe along the sides *(Fig. 1)*. Remove the tape.

Fig. 1

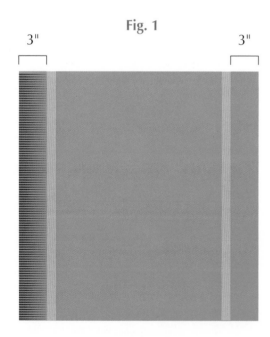

2. Wrap the pillow fleece piece around the pillow form and secure at the ends with rubber bands.
3. Tie a 1½" x 12" contrasting fleece strip over each rubber band.

Yellow Round Pillow

Approximate Finished Size:
14" diameter, excluding fringe

SHOPPING LIST

- ☐ two 24" fleece squares
- ☐ 14" round pillow form
- ☐ masking tape
- ☐ fabric marker
- ☐ thumbtack
- ☐ string

To make the pillow:

1. Match the **right** sides and fold one 24" fleece square in half from top to bottom and again from left to right. Tie one end of a length of string to the fabric marker; insert a thumbtack through the string at 11". Insert the thumbtack through the folded fleece corner. Holding the tack in place and keeping the string taut, mark the cutting line *(Fig. 1)*. Cut out the circle. Use this circle as a pattern to cut the remaining fleece square.

Fig. 1

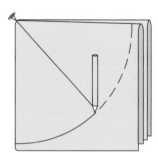

2. Stack the fleece pieces **wrong** sides together. Place masking tape strips 4" in from the circle edge. Cutting through both layers, cut 1" wide x 4" deep fringe along the edge of each fleece circle *(Fig. 2)*. Remove the tape.

3. Using one fringe strip from each fleece piece and tying each knot twice, tie knots around most of the pillow. Insert the pillow form in the pillow and tie the remaining fringe strips.

Fig. 2

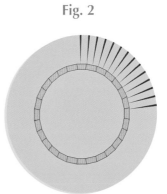

Fishing Throw

Approximate Finished Size: 52" x 60", excluding fringe

SHOPPING LIST

- ☐ 1³/₄ yards **each** of 2 contrasting fleeces
- ☐ five 12" x 22" pieces of contrasting fleece for fringe on top and bottom
- ☐ masking tape

To make the throw:

1. Cut a 56" x 60" piece of both the large fleece pieces. Stack the fleece pieces **wrong** sides together.
2. Place masking tape strips 2" in from the side edges. Cutting through both layers, cut ¹/₂" wide x 2" deep fringe along the sides of each fleece piece **(Fig. 1)**. Remove the tape.

Fig. 1

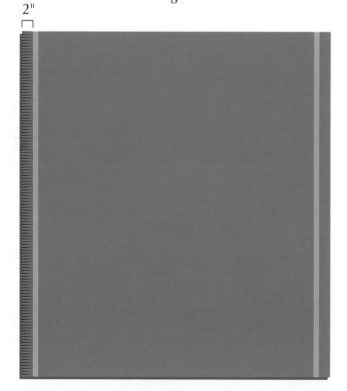

3. Using one fringe strip from each fleece piece, tie twisted knots (page 30) to join the front and back along the sides.
4. Cutting through both layers, make ¹/₂" long horizontal slits along the top and bottom edges approximately ¹/₂" apart **(Fig. 2)**.

Fig. 2

5. For the contrasting fringe, cut 20 1" x 10" fringe strips from **each** fringe fleece piece.
6. Use the fringe strips to join the top and bottom edges, making a lark's head knot (page 30) through each horizontal slit.

Duvet Cover

Approximate Finished Size: 90" x 96", excluding fringe (fits a full/queen-sized duvet)

To make the cover:

1. For the duvet cover front, cut a 58" wide x 99" long fleece piece and two 25" wide x 99" long fleece pieces.

2. Matching the **wrong** sides, stack the fleece pieces together. Place masking tape strips 3" in from the side and bottom edges. Cutting through both layers, cut ¹/₂" wide x 3" deep fringe along the side and bottom edges of each fleece piece *(Fig. 1)*.

Fig. 1

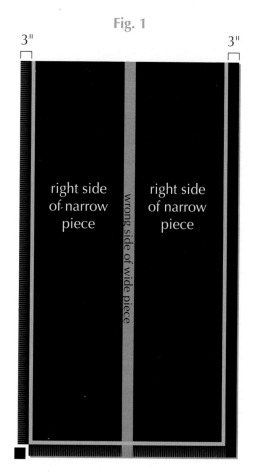

3. Using one fringe strip from each fleece piece, tie twisted knots (page 30) along the side edges to complete the cover front.

Continued on page 18.

4. For the duvet cover back, cut two 51" wide x 111" long fleece pieces.

5. Stack the fleece pieces *wrong* sides together. Place a masking tape strip 3" in from the side and bottom edges. Leaving 12" uncut on *the side only*, cut ½" wide x 3" deep fringe along the side, center, and bottom edges of each fleece piece *(Fig. 2)*.

Fig. 2

6. Using one fringe strip from each fleece piece, tie twisted knots along the center to complete the cover back.

7. Matching the *wrong* sides, tie the front and back together along the side and bottom edges, leaving the top open to insert the duvet. Insert the duvet and fold the top back extension to the inside.

Other Bed Sizes:

Twin *(finished size: 68" x 86", excluding fringe)*
5 yards of fleece for the front and 5¾ yards of fleece for the back; cut one front piece 46" wide x 89" long and two front pieces 20" wide x 89" long; cut the back pieces 40" wide x 101" long

King *(finished size: 99" x 96", excluding fringe)*
5⅝ yards of fleece for the front and 6¼ yards of fleece for the back; cut one front piece 59" wide x 99" long and two front pieces 29" wide x 99" long; cut the back pieces 55½" wide x 111" long

Pillowcases

Approximate Finished Size:
20" x 32" (fits a standard 20" x 26" bed pillow)

SHOPPING LIST

- ☐ 1½ yards of fleece for two pillowcases
- ☐ four 9" x 25" pieces of contrasting fleece for borders
- ☐ masking tape

To make each pillowcase:

1. Cut a 55" x 25" fleece piece from the pillowcase fleece.
2. Matching the **right** sides, stack two border fleece pieces on the short ends of the pillowcase piece. Place masking tape strips 2½" in from the side edges. Cutting through both layers, cut ¾" wide x 2½" deep fringe on the ends of each fleece piece *(Fig. 1)*. Remove the tape.

Fig. 1

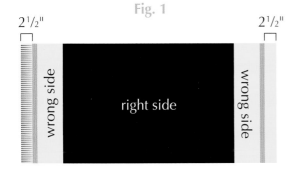

3. Using one fringe strip from each fleece piece, tie twisted knots (page 30) to join the borders to each short end of the pillowcase piece.

4. Matching the borders and the **right** sides, fold the pillowcase in half. Place masking tape strips 2½" in from the top and bottom edges. Cutting through both layers, cut ¾" wide x 2½" deep fringe on each fleece piece *(Fig. 2)*, cutting off the previously tied knots in the fringe areas. Remove the tape.

Fig. 2

5. Tie twisted knots at the top and bottom. Turn right side out so that the knots are inside the pillowcase.
6. Repeat Steps 1-5 to make the remaining pillowcase.

Houndstooth Pillow

Approximate Finished Size: 24" square, excluding fringe

SHOPPING LIST

- ☐ two 30" fleece squares
- ☐ 24" square pillow form
- ☐ masking tape

To make the pillow:

1. Stack the fleece pieces **wrong** sides together.
2. Place masking tape strips 3" in from all four sides. Cutting through both layers, cut ³⁄₄" wide x 3" deep fringe along all four sides of each fleece piece *(Fig. 1)*. Remove the tape.

Fig. 1

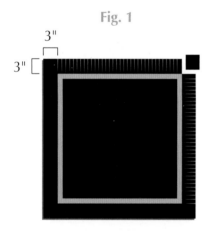

3. Using one fringe strip from each fleece piece and tying each knot twice, tie knots along three sides. Insert the pillow form and tie the fourth side.

Black Flower Pillow

Approximate Finished Size: 14" diameter

SHOPPING LIST

- ☐ 34" fleece square for pillow
- ☐ 14" x 22" fleece piece for petals
- ☐ 54" x 3" fleece piece for ruffle
- ☐ 14" round pillow form
- ☐ fabric marker
- ☐ thumbtack
- ☐ rubber band
- ☐ hot glue gun and glue sticks
- ☐ tracing paper
- ☐ string

To make the pillow:

1. For the flower, match the **right** sides and fold the 34" fleece square in half from top to bottom and again from left to right. Tie one end of a length of string to the fabric marker; insert a thumbtack through the string at 16". Insert the thumbtack through the folded fleece corner. Holding the tack in place and keeping the string taut, mark the cutting line *(Fig. 1)*. Cut out the circle.

Fig. 1

2. Center the pillow form on the wrong side of the fleece circle. Gather the fleece around the pillow form and secure with the rubber band *(Photo 1)*.

3. Trace the large petal pattern (page 32) onto tracing paper and cut out. Use the pattern to cut 10 petals. Pleating the straight edges of the petals, hot glue the petals to the pillow *(Photo 2)*.

4. Hot glue the ruffle fleece piece to the pillow, pleating it as you glue.

Photo 1

Photo 2

Frog Throw

Approximate Finished Size: 31¹/₂" x 53¹/₂", excluding fringe

SHOPPING LIST

- ☐ 1³/₄ yards of fleece
- ☐ masking tape

To make the throw:

1. Cut the fleece to 37" x 59".
2. Place masking tape strips 2³/₄" in from all four sides of the fleece piece. Cut 1" wide x 2³/₄" deep fringe along all four sides of the fleece piece *(Fig. 1)*.

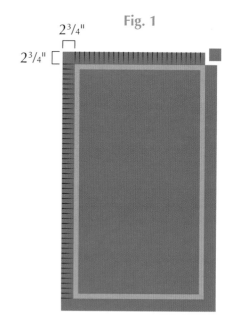

Fig. 1

2³/₄"
2³/₄"

3. Trim each fringe strip to a point and cut a 1" long slit in the fringe 1¹/₂" above the point *(Fig. 2)*.

Fig. 2

4. Fold a fringe point up and pull it through the slit *(Fig. 3)*. Repeat around the entire throw.

Fig. 3

Scalloped Throw

Approximate Finished Size: 37" x 52"

SHOPPING LIST

- ☐ 1½ yards of fleece for throw
- ☐ ¼ yard of contrasting fleece for "ribbon"
- ☐ fabric marker
- ☐ tracing paper

To make the throw:

1. Cut a 37" x 52" fleece piece. Trace the scallop pattern (page 32) onto tracing paper and cut out. Starting at a corner and repeating the scallops along the edges, use the pattern to cut the scallops and "ribbon" slits around the throw edges.

2. Cut four 1¼" wide strips across the width of the fleece for the "ribbons." Thread the strips through the slits and tie the ends together at the corners. Trim the strip ends.

Camo Throw

Approximate Finished Size: 50" x 75", excluding fringe

SHOPPING LIST

- ☐ 2³⁄₄ yards **each** of 2 contrasting fleeces
- ☐ masking tape

To make the throw:

1. Cut three 31" squares from each fleece piece.
2. Place masking tape strips 3" in from all four sides on a fleece square. Cut ⁵⁄₈" wide x 3" deep fringe along all four sides *(Fig. 1)*. Repeat on the remaining five fleece squares, making the same number of cuts on all sides of all squares. Remove the tape.

Fig. 1

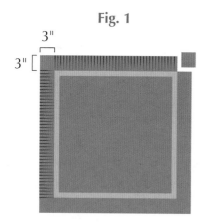

3. Referring to the diagram, use twisted knots (page 30) to tie the squares together, first in rows and then to join the rows.

Diagram

Camo Pillow

Approximate Finished Size: 16" square, excluding fringe

SHOPPING LIST

- ☐ 22" square **each** of 2 contrasting fleeces
- ☐ 16" square pillow form
- ☐ masking tape

To make the pillow:

1. Stack the fleece squares **wrong** sides together.
2. Place masking tape strips 3" in from all four sides. Cutting through both layers, cut ³⁄₄" wide x 3" deep fringe along all four sides of each fleece piece *(Fig. 1)*. Remove the tape.

Fig. 1

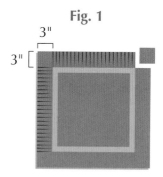

3. Using one fringe strip from each fleece piece, tie twisted knots (page 30) around three sides of the pillow. Insert the pillow form and tie the fourth side.

Flamingo Throw

Approximate Finished Size: 57" x 78"

SHOPPING LIST

- ☐ 2 yards of fleece for throw
- ☐ two 57" x 12" pieces of contrasting fleece for borders
- ☐ masking tape

To make the throw:

1. Cut the large fleece piece to 57" x 70".
2. Matching the **wrong** sides, stack the border fleece pieces on the short ends of the large fleece piece. Place masking tape strips 4" in from the short ends. Cutting through both layers, cut ³/₄" wide x 4" deep fringe on the ends of each fleece piece *(Fig. 1)*. Remove the tape.

Fig. 1

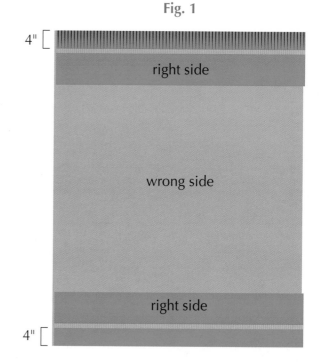

4" [

right side

wrong side

right side

4" [

3. Using one fringe strip from each fleece piece, tie twisted knots (page 30) to join the borders to the throw.

Yellow Flower Pillow

Approximate Finished Size: 12" x 24"

SHOPPING LIST

- ☐ 24" x 27" fleece piece for pillow
- ☐ 17" fleece square for bottom layer of petals
- ☐ 13" fleece square for middle layer of petals
- ☐ 9" fleece square for top layer of petals
- ☐ 8" fleece square for leaves
- ☐ fleece scrap for flower center
- ☐ 22" x 12" pillow form
- ☐ hot glue gun and glue sticks
- ☐ tracing paper

Fig. 1

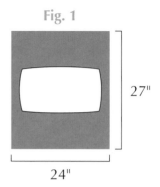

27"

24"

To make the pillow:

1. Center the pillow form on the wrong side of the pillow fleece *(Fig. 1)*. Fold the short ends over the pillow form. Overlap and hot glue at the center. Hot glue the side edges closed.

2. For the bottom layer petals, freehand cut an irregular $7^{1}/_{2}$" fleece circle. Cut 3 more circles, each just slightly smaller than the last one.

3. For the middle layer petals, freehand cut an irregular 6" fleece circle. Cut 2 more circles, each just slightly smaller than the last one.

4. For the top layer petals, freehand cut an irregular 4" fleece circle. Cut 2 more circles, each slightly smaller than the last one.

5. For the flower center, cut five $^{3}/_{8}$" x 4" fleece strips. Knot each strip at the center and trim the fleece tails close to the knot.

6. Trace the leaf patterns (page 31) onto tracing paper and cut out. Use the patterns to cut the leaves.

7. Referring to the photo, hot glue the petal circles (gluing the centers only), flower center knots, and leaves to the pillow.

White Flower Pillow

Approximate Finished Size: 14" diameter

SHOPPING LIST

- ☐ 34" fleece square for pillow
- ☐ ½ yard of fleece for petals
- ☐ 6" x 12" fleece piece for flower centers
- ☐ 14" round pillow form
- ☐ fabric marker
- ☐ thumbtack
- ☐ rubber band
- ☐ hot glue gun and glue sticks
- ☐ tracing paper
- ☐ string

Photo 1

To make the pillow:

1. For the flower, match the right sides and fold the 34" fleece square in half from top to bottom and again from left to right. Tie one end of a length of string to the fabric marker; insert a thumbtack through the string at 16". Insert the thumbtack through the folded fleece corner. Holding the tack in place and keeping the string taut, mark the cutting line *(Fig. 1)*. Cut out the circle.

Fig. 1

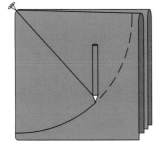

2. Center the pillow form on the wrong side of the fleece circle. Gather the fleece around the pillow form and secure with the rubber band *(Photo 1)*.

3. Trace the petal patterns (page 32) onto tracing paper and cut out. Use the patterns to cut 21 large petals and 8 small petals. Pleating the straight edges of the petals, hot glue the petals to the pillow, starting with the large petals for the bottom layer *(Photo 2)*; continue pleating and gluing, using the large petals for the middle layer and the small petals for the top layer.

Photo 2

4. For the flower centers, cut eight 1¼" x 5" fleece strips. Loosely knot each strip at the center and trim the tails close to the knot. Hot glue the knots between the fleece folds.

Knots

LARK'S HEAD KNOT

Fold the strip in half and pull the loop through the fleece from front to back; pull the ends through the loop and tighten the knot *(Figs. 1-2)*.

Fig. 1

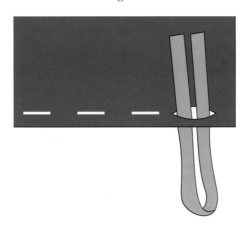

Fig. 2

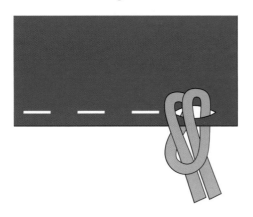

TWISTED KNOT

Because this knot is twisted before you tie the second time, the contrasting fringe shows up well against the project. Stack the fleece pieces ***wrong*** sides together, unless otherwise indicated. Using one fringe strip from each fleece piece, tie a knot *(Fig. 3)*. Twist the fringe strips clockwise *(Fig. 4)* and tie another knot *(Fig. 5)*. Continue tying twisted knots to join the pieces.

Fig. 3

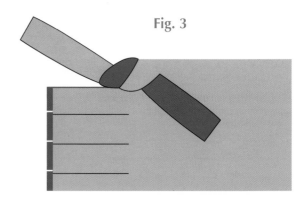

Fig. 4

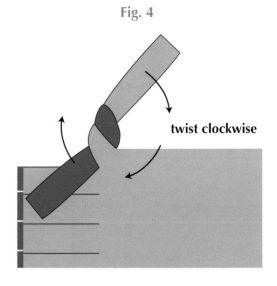

twist clockwise

Fig. 5

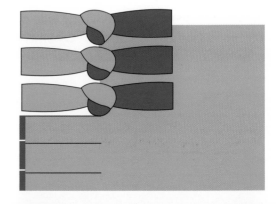

Patterns

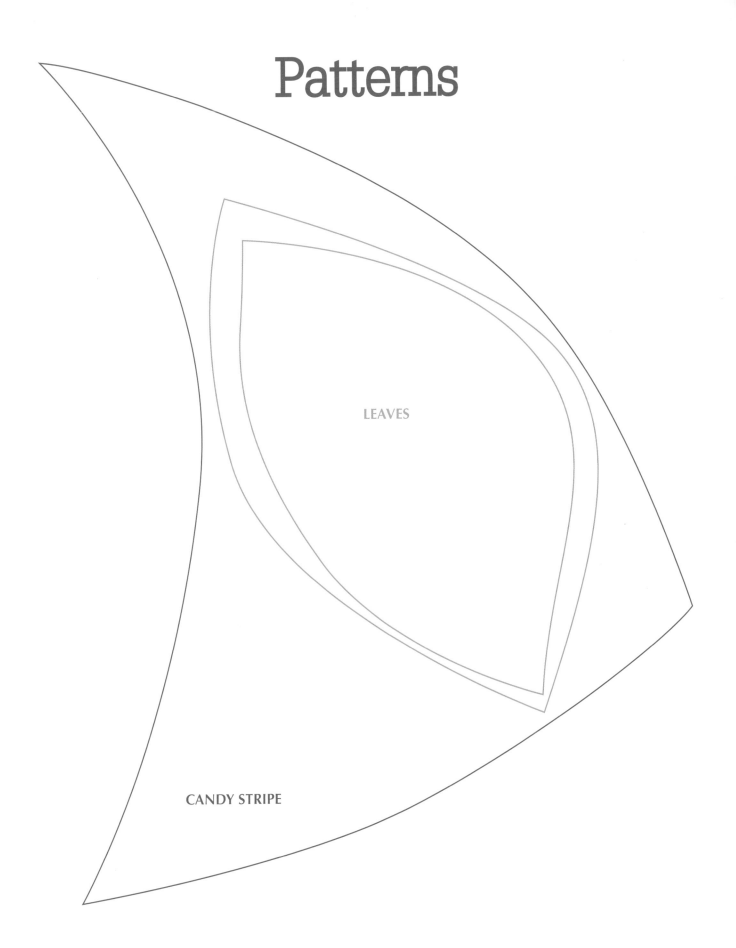

LEAVES

CANDY STRIPE

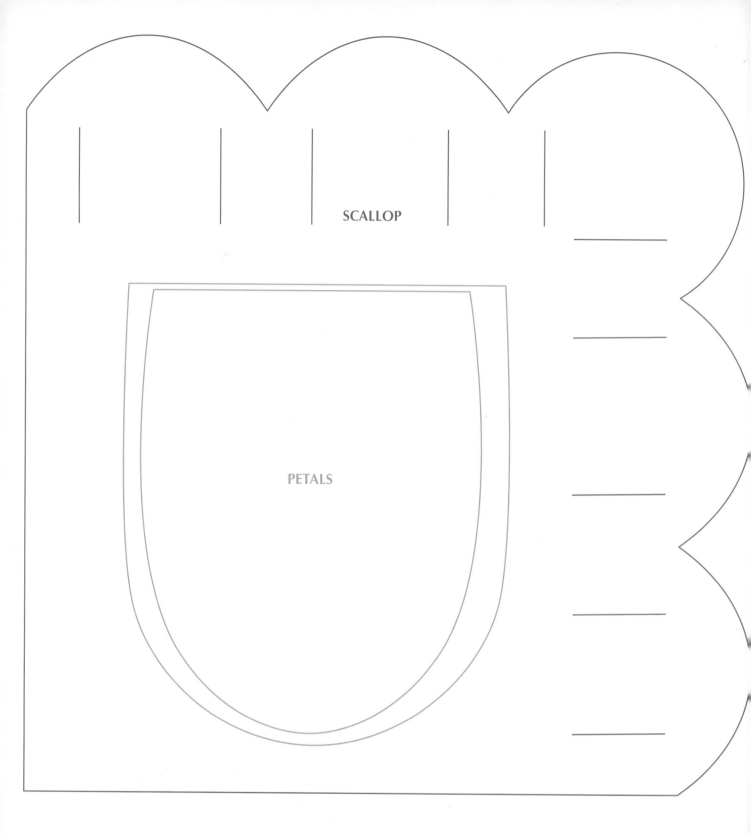

SCALLOP

PETALS

Production Team: Designer – Patti Wallenfang; Design Assistant – Kelly Reider; Technical Writer – Mary Sullivan Hutcheson; Technical Assistants – Lisa Lancaster and Jean Lewis; Editorial Writer – Susan Frantz Wiles; Senior Graphic Artist – Lora Puls; Graphic Artist – Kara Darling; Photo Stylist – Christy Myers; Photographers – Mark Matthews and Ken West